WAYS
OF
DRAWING
Faces
AND PORTRAITS

" Day after day,
never fail to draw something
which, however little it may be,
will yet in the end be much, **"**
and do thy best.

Cennino Cennini c.1390

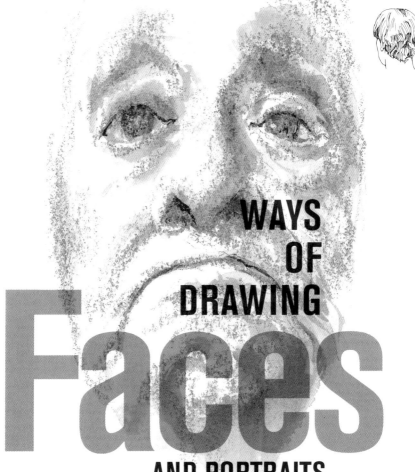

WAYS
OF
DRAWING
Faces
AND PORTRAITS

A guide to expanding your visual awareness

CASSELL

WAYS OF DRAWING FACES AND PORTRAITS,
a guide to expanding your visual awareness

Copyright © 1995 by Inklink

This edition first published in Great Britain 1996 by Studio Vista an imprint of the Cassell group

British Library Cataloguing in Publication Data
A catalogue record for this book is available from the British Library

ISBN 0-289-80160-5

Produced, edited, and designed by Inklink,
Greenwich, London, England.

CONSULTANT ARTISTS AND EDITORIAL BOARD
Concept and general editor, Simon Jennings
Contributing artist, Valerie Wiffen
Art-education advisor, Carolynn Cooke
Design and art direction, Simon Jennings
Text editors, Ian Kearey and Albert Jackson
Historical research, Ella Jennings and Peter Anderson

Typeset in Akzidenz Grotesque, Bodoni, and Univers by Inklink
Printed by South Sea International Press, Hong Kong

Cassell Publishers Limited
Wellington House, 125 Strand
London WC2R 0BB

CONTENTS

Head of an elderly woman
Sepia brush and wash.

The key to success in drawing portraits is to follow a simple, four-stage process. **The first** is learning to look carefully at your model: casual glances gather little information and leave no memory.

Next, select what you feel is important from the immense amount of visual information in front of you, deciding how much to incorporate and whether you intend to simplify the drawing or work it up with a lot of detail. This, in turn, will give you a clue as to how large the work should be.

Stage three is making actual marks or brushstrokes on a sympathetic surface, usually paper. Making marks and lines, and applying areas of tone or washes – the physical act of drawing – initially demand a great deal of attention from an artist. However, looking and choosing are just as vital, and the marks you make will only fall into place and create a plausible image if they are grounded in good observation. Look at least as much as you draw, if not more!

The last stage is to check your marks and make sure they really represent what you have seen and chosen. Too thin? Too dark? Wrong angle? Change them right away, because a successful drawing depends upon the relationships between the various elements on the paper, and to misrepresent one part will distort others. A critical faculty is required; compare your work to your subject in order to ensure that each new touch adds to the sound core of accurate marks already made. If something doesn't work, change it immediately. The ability to appraise and revise a drawing is an essential skill to develop, and will make you truly independent as an artist.

The anatomy of the face The human skull has a whole range of functions beyond mere protection, all of which influence its structure and proportions. As an artist, you will find that a basic knowledge of the bones that underpin the physiognomy, and the muscles lying on top of them, will help you convey the character of any model.

The main features of the skull are the mandible, or lower jaw, and the cranium. The upper part of the cranium, called the calvaria, forms a box that encloses and protects the brain. The remainder of the skull forms the facial skeleton, of which the upper part is immovably fixed to the calvaria, and the lower part forms the freely movable mandible.

Although the skull determines the overall shape of the head, it is, in fact, the

Background
Detail from *Anatomie de l'Homme*, by Jules Cloquet (*fl.* 19th century).

37

muscles that lie beneath the skin of the face, scalp, and neck that create the facial expressions that give movement and character to each individual.

While it is helpful to be aware of the many muscles responsible for lip movements, and those that surround the cavity of each eye, the problem confronting you as a portraitist is that all this underlying structure is hidden beneath layers of hair, skin, and fleshy features. As an artist, you must rely on close observation to determine how much of what you know lies beneath the surface actually shows in the face you are drawing. The same attention to detail will enable you to record the huge range of emotions revealed by slight movements of facial muscles, and depict subtleties, such as mood and temperament.

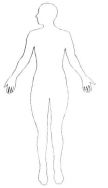

Head size and proportions
In general, the size of the head is divisible into the total height of the person by eight.

Facial proportions
The bottoms of the eye sockets are halfway up the head.

Artists should rely on direct observation in coming to terms with the unique appearance and particular characteristics of each individual, whatever their race, age, or sex.

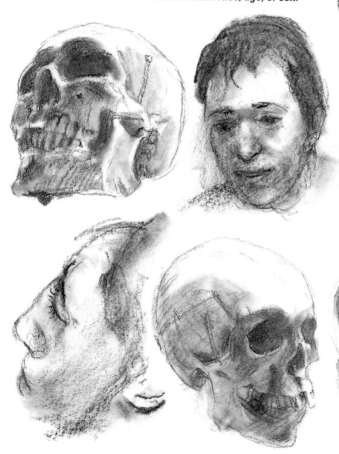

• PARTS OF THE SKULL

• Cranium
The whole skull, except for the jawbone.

• Calvaria
The rounded "cap" of the skull.

• Superciliary arch
This bony ridge is visible just below the eyebrows. In elderly models, the entire eye socket can sometimes be made out.

• Zygomatic bone
Also known as the cheekbone, this is most obvious in a half-profile view.

• Mandible
The movable lower jaw includes the chin.

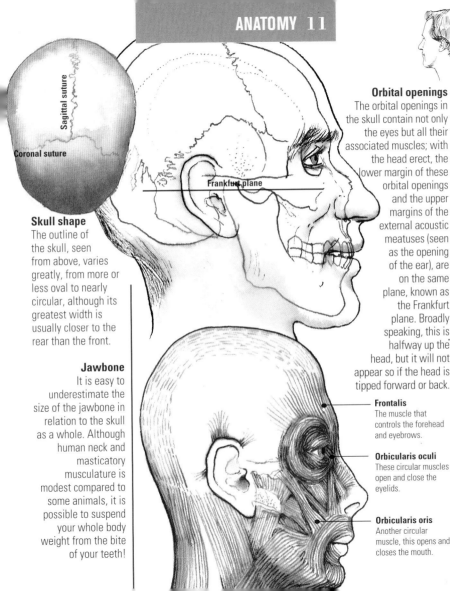

Sagittal suture

Coronal suture

Skull shape
The outline of the skull, seen from above, varies greatly, from more or less oval to nearly circular, although its greatest width is usually closer to the rear than the front.

Jawbone
It is easy to underestimate the size of the jawbone in relation to the skull as a whole. Although human neck and masticatory musculature is modest compared to some animals, it is possible to suspend your whole body weight from the bite of your teeth!

Frankfurt plane

Orbital openings
The orbital openings in the skull contain not only the eyes but all their associated muscles; with the head erect, the lower margin of these orbital openings and the upper margins of the external acoustic meatuses (seen as the opening of the ear), are on the same plane, known as the Frankfurt plane. Broadly speaking, this is halfway up the head, but it will not appear so if the head is tipped forward or back.

Frontalis
The muscle that controls the forehead and eyebrows.

Orbicularis oculi
These circular muscles open and close the eyelids.

Orbicularis oris
Another circular muscle, this opens and closes the mouth.

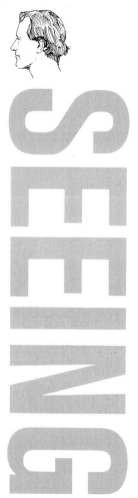

SEEING

Background
Detail from *Iconographic Encyclopaedia*, 1851, by J.G. Heck.

When driving down the road, we take the broad view so that we are aware of the child who may run out in front of the car, the woman waiting on the sidewalk, or the truck that may pull out suddenly. In contrast, when threading a needle, or hammering a nail, we take a very specific view, focused on the task in hand.

To make a successful drawing, it is important to start with the driver's view and scan broadly to encompass the whole of your chosen image. The focused view comes later. And just like the busy driver who must be able to maintain control by reacting automatically to what is happening all around, it is important to develop the ability to observe and draw at the same time.

Starting up means choosing your viewpoint (something most of us have experienced when looking through the finder of a camera), deciding whether you want to depict just the face, the head alone, the head and shoulders, or perhaps a half-length portrait that includes the clothed or nude torso. Much depends on how the model inspires you, and how you think you could best convey the unique character of this particular human being. You might find that making a few preparatory sketches will help you begin to see what is interesting about your subject, or perhaps taking a series of photographs from every angle will help focus your mind.

Part of the same process is to decide on the format. Although a vertical support is known as the "portrait" view, for some subjects the horizontal, "landscape," mode may give you a more interesting result by providing scope for a better design.

Keep your distance
Remember to stand back once in a while and look from a little distance, where the detail that is so preoccupying at close quarters can have a very different effect.

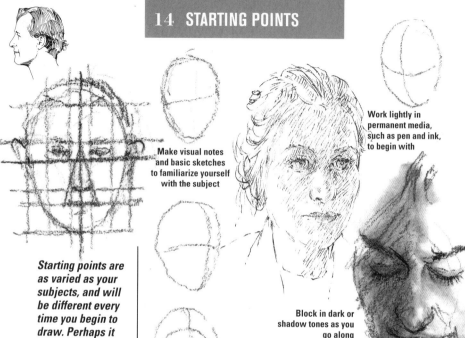

Make visual notes and basic sketches to familiarize yourself with the subject

Work lightly in permanent media, such as pen and ink, to begin with

Block in dark or shadow tones as you go along

Starting points are as varied as your subjects, and will be different every time you begin to draw. Perhaps it will be the angle of a nose, the shape of a shadow across a cheek, a diagonal strand of hair – any of these could be the right place to start. Just look for something that you know you can set down relatively accurately, without any other reference points to guide you.

Basic construction
Solve any problems of perspective or proportion before going for full-strength marks and specific details. Once you have achieved a sound framework, the details will fall into place naturally.

Broad strokes
It sometimes helps to block in the main areas of tone. If you are working in an erasable medium (one you can rub out), blocking in the dark or shadow tones as you go along enables you to get a feel for the three-dimensional nature of what you are drawing.

A light touch
When using ink, wash, or any other medium you can't erase once you've applied it to the paper, you may prefer to start with a diluted ink, or use very light touches until you are sure you have your drawing organized as you want.

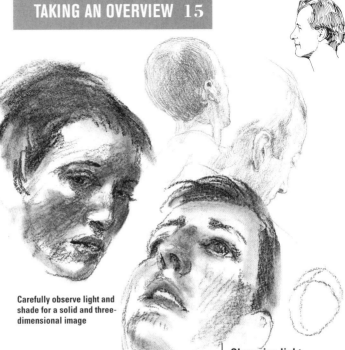

When most people find themselves face to face with another human being, they are automatically drawn to make eye contact. The same reaction often encourages an artist to begin a portrait by drawing the eyes – perhaps one of the hardest ways to get going. Resist the temptation to concentrate on the details at the expense of the overview. If in doubt, always go for the larger option, like the overall shape of the head. Look for the relationship between the various planes of the person's features until you have created a solid core upon which to build.

Carefully observe light and shade for a solid and three-dimensional image

Drawing lines and tones

A lot of problems are caused by drawing lines round the edges of objects; this makes it very difficult to keep things in proportion. In any case, features such as noses and lips aren't really defined by lines. What we see as a line is merely the "horizon," as a curved surface disappears from view. Unless you are deliberately making a line-only drawing (which is notoriously difficult), try building up tones by working across the forms, including lines if and when they are needed. Working this way will teach you to use linework to describe three-dimensional items instead of surrounding them.

Observing light and shade

Look especially for the fall of light across the head and surfaces of the face. Depicting this play of light and shade will give you a convincingly solid and realistic image of the person. Once you have this, adjusting proportions to catch a likeness becomes much easier.

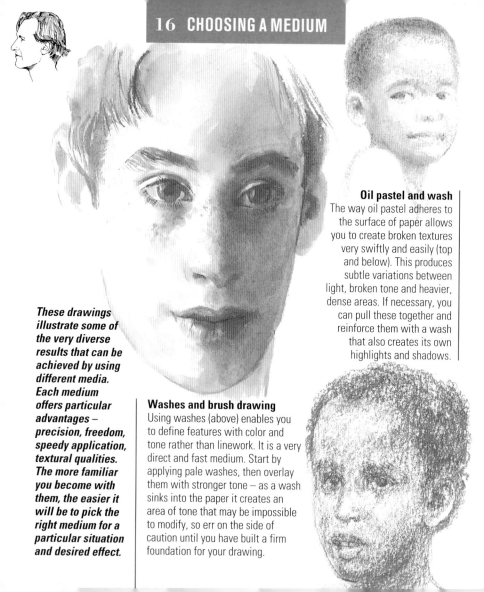

These drawings illustrate some of the very diverse results that can be achieved by using different media. Each medium offers particular advantages – precision, freedom, speedy application, textural qualities. The more familiar you become with them, the easier it will be to pick the right medium for a particular situation and desired effect.

Oil pastel and wash
The way oil pastel adheres to the surface of paper allows you to create broken textures very swiftly and easily (top and below). This produces subtle variations between light, broken tone and heavier, dense areas. If necessary, you can pull these together and reinforce them with a wash that also creates its own highlights and shadows.

Washes and brush drawing
Using washes (above) enables you to define features with color and tone rather than linework. It is a very direct and fast medium. Start by applying pale washes, then overlay them with stronger tone – as a wash sinks into the paper it creates an area of tone that may be impossible to modify, so err on the side of caution until you have built a firm foundation for your drawing.

Pencil and ink drawings

Graphite pencil (right) or pen and ink (below left) work best when a model is prepared to sit still for a long time. Alternatively, use them to make finished drawings from preliminary sketches or photographs. Both media produce linear marks, which can be used to follow the curve of a cheek or create the texture of fine hair.

Pastel and paper stump

Pastel drawing (below right) is affected by the texture of the paper and by how you use the pastel: drawing with the side of a pastel stick will produce wide areas of tone, while using the tip makes smaller, more intense marks. You can use a paper stump, also called a torchon or tortillon, to blend and soften pastel and other soft-media drawings.

Some artists use a sketchbook to put down visual notes which will form the basis for more finished work later. Others enjoy sketching for its own sake, creating fresh, uninhibited drawings. Use an eraser if you must, but it is far better to wade in, go for it, and make a series of drawings that are far more informative than a labored rendering made under less-than-perfect circumstances.

Locations

Street corners, markets, and playgrounds are particularly good places for sketching. Because the majority of people will be engrossed in their own activities, you will be able to draw them in unselfconscious poses.

Carrying on
People are always on the move. If you are sketching someone sipping tea in a café, don't be surprised if they drink up and go before you have finished. Just look for another person and start again; even unfinished drawings are useful references.

Preserving your anonymity
Try using a small sketchbook if you want to draw unobserved; most people will assume that you're writing a postcard or making a shopping list, and will hardly notice you. Carry it everywhere with you, and sketch wherever you can.

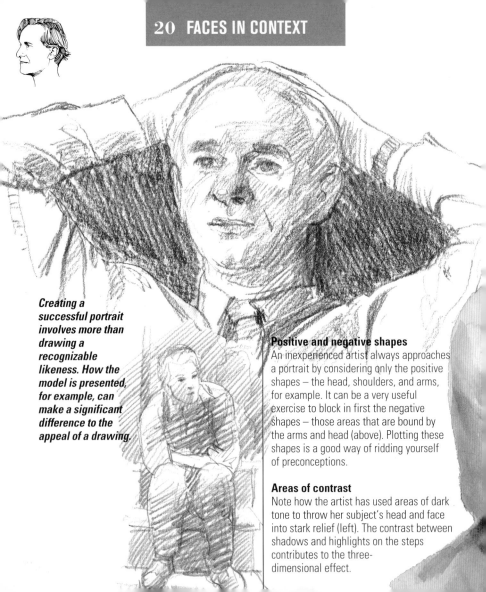

Creating a successful portrait involves more than drawing a recognizable likeness. How the model is presented, for example, can make a significant difference to the appeal of a drawing.

Positive and negative shapes

An inexperienced artist always approaches a portrait by considering only the positive shapes – the head, shoulders, and arms, for example. It can be a very useful exercise to block in first the negative shapes – those areas that are bound by the arms and head (above). Plotting these shapes is a good way of ridding yourself of preconceptions.

Areas of contrast

Note how the artist has used areas of dark tone to throw her subject's head and face into stark relief (left). The contrast between shadows and highlights on the steps contributes to the three-dimensional effect.

Framing the face
An all-embracing garment, such as this hooded coat (below), focuses our attention on the model's features. Framing a face often adds strength to a portrait, accentuating those areas that catch the prevailing light.

Looking for angles
Some lines in this ink-and-wash drawing (right) have been emphasized to stress the rhythm they bring to the composition. Repetition of this sort contributes a dynamic strength to the work.

Because we instinctively use eye contact as a means of communication, many artists tend to over-estimate the importance of eyes in comparison to the rest of the face when drawing. This can result in the eyes being out of proportion, for example, or becoming overworked and fussy.

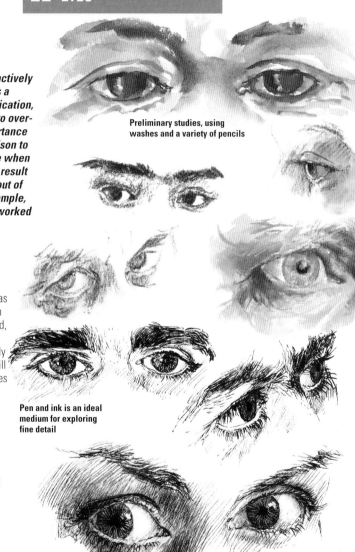

Preliminary studies, using washes and a variety of pencils

Pairs of eyes
Make sure that both eyes track together as a pair. Depending on the angle of the head, the positions of the irises may not exactly correspond, but it will be obvious when eyes do not appear to be focusing together.

Pen and ink is an ideal medium for exploring fine detail

Reflected light
Accurate placing of reflected light in the eyes is absolutely essential (right), and should be related to the position of the actual light source.

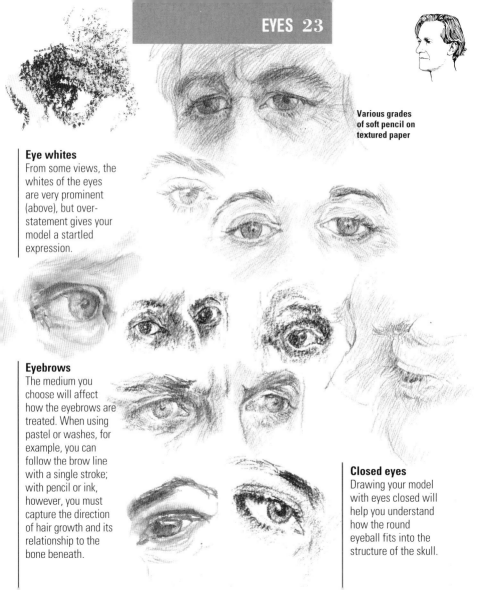

Various grades of soft pencil on textured paper

Eye whites
From some views, the whites of the eyes are very prominent (above), but over-statement gives your model a startled expression.

Eyebrows
The medium you choose will affect how the eyebrows are treated. When using pastel or washes, for example, you can follow the brow line with a single stroke; with pencil or ink, however, you must capture the direction of hair growth and its relationship to the bone beneath.

Closed eyes
Drawing your model with eyes closed will help you understand how the round eyeball fits into the structure of the skull.

Inexperienced artists are often anxious about drawing noses. Experiment with materials, techniques, and viewpoints to show how a nose stands out from the face. Here and opposite we see a variety of techniques in use: watercolor wash, bold pastel, and fine pencil line.

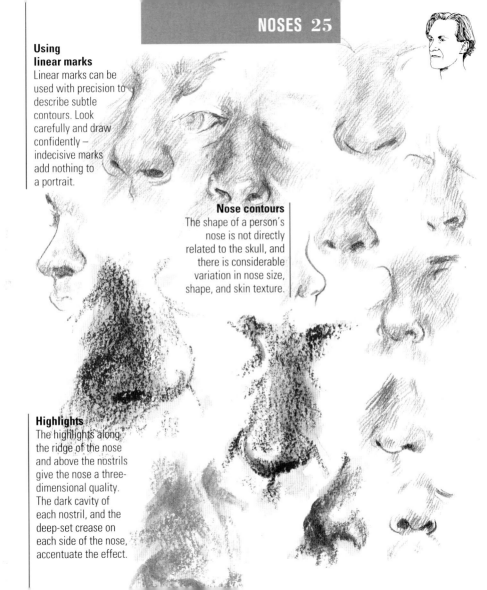

Using linear marks

Linear marks can be used with precision to describe subtle contours. Look carefully and draw confidently – indecisive marks add nothing to a portrait.

Nose contours

The shape of a person's nose is not directly related to the skull, and there is considerable variation in nose size, shape, and skin texture.

Highlights

The highlights along the ridge of the nose and above the nostrils give the nose a three-dimensional quality. The dark cavity of each nostril, and the deep-set crease on each side of the nose, accentuate the effect.

The mouth is extraordinarily expressive, and is a remarkable vehicle for conveying the model's character. An accurate portrayal of the mouth, within the overall shape of the face, is a key factor in catching a likeness.

Not all mouths are symmetrical
Don't assume that a person's lips are perfectly regular. The asymmetrical or lopsided nature of some mouths is both fascinating and a challenge to draw.

Pencil drawings
Because graphite pencil is so expressive, it can be used to suggest a variety of textures.

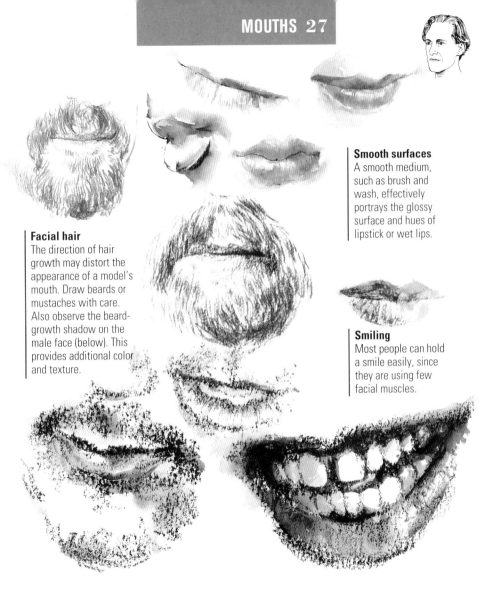

Facial hair
The direction of hair growth may distort the appearance of a model's mouth. Draw beards or mustaches with care. Also observe the beard-growth shadow on the male face (below). This provides additional color and texture.

Smooth surfaces
A smooth medium, such as brush and wash, effectively portrays the glossy surface and hues of lipstick or wet lips.

Smiling
Most people can hold a smile easily, since they are using few facial muscles.

Because they are so complex, drawing ears is often one of the more difficult aspects of portraiture. Each person's ears are so distinctive, they demand careful consideration if you want to achieve a convincing likeness.

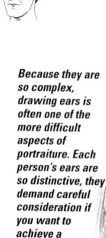

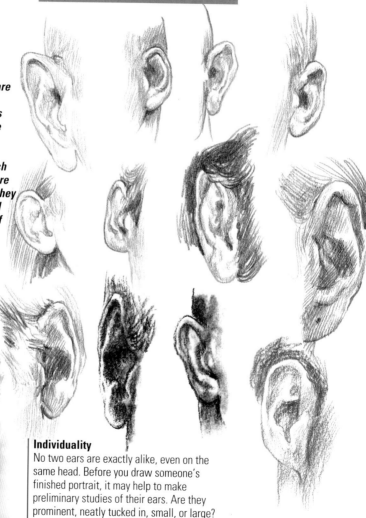

Individuality

No two ears are exactly alike, even on the same head. Before you draw someone's finished portrait, it may help to make preliminary studies of their ears. Are they prominent, neatly tucked in, small, or large?

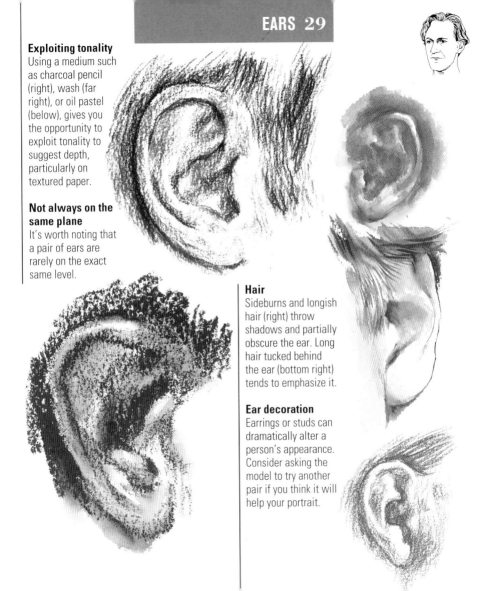

Exploiting tonality
Using a medium such as charcoal pencil (right), wash (far right), or oil pastel (below), gives you the opportunity to exploit tonality to suggest depth, particularly on textured paper.

Not always on the same plane
It's worth noting that a pair of ears are rarely on the exact same level.

Hair
Sideburns and longish hair (right) throw shadows and partially obscure the ear. Long hair tucked behind the ear (bottom right) tends to emphasize it.

Ear decoration
Earrings or studs can dramatically alter a person's appearance. Consider asking the model to try another pair if you think it will help your portrait.

Drawing hair is fun since it is a tremendously varied subject, and presents all sorts of technical and artistic challenges. The one thing you don't want is to produce a three-dimensional face and then to flatten the whole effect by drawing two-dimensional hair. The correct choice of medium can be crucial in this artistic process.

Soft-charcoal pencil

Dark hair
Even in very dark hair, (left) there are cast shadows and highlights that help describe the form.

Hair styles
Hair can be piled up, cut, or fluffed out in many different ways (opposite), but whatever the style, make sure the hair relates to the basic skull shape beneath.

Pen, ink, and wash

Using two media
Here the artist used a wash to block in the mass of head hair (left), then overlaid it with pen and ink to suggest fine strands over the forehead and around the ear. If a medium enables you to represent what you see quickly and easily, and with more veracity than any other, then that is the medium to use.

Drawing long hair
One way to depict long, shiny hair (below) is to apply a dragged wash, using a slightly damp brush. The artist knew that the fine bristles on the brush would splay out to create the linear shadow effect, and that long brush-strokes would mimic the flowing hair style.

Hard-charcoal pencil

There is as much variety among babies and small children as among adults; they come in all shapes and sizes, and each is an individual. Don't fall into obvious preconceptions about young facial features or proportions, but observe closely and make lots of sketches.

Point of emphasis
The relationship of parent to child is an important element in this composition (left). To focus attention on the baby, the mother's face is drawn in full, heavy shadow.

The right medium
Trying to draw a wriggling three-year-old with a pencil can be a thankless task; it is often better to choose a medium, such as a wash or charcoal, with which you can achieve a wide range of tones freely and quickly.

Children's eyes
The lack of pouches and wrinkles around the eyes of a young child makes them stand out against the clear skin. This has the effect of drawing attention to them.

Instantly recognizable
The proportions of a child's face are noticeably different from those of an adult, even when most of the facial features are hidden.

Asleep or awake
Sleeping babies are the easiest to draw; more active children may only be caught on paper by a series of sketches. It is often worth arranging to work with a child over several sittings, and then use the results to produce a finished drawing later.

Changing shape
The shape of a baby's skull is very different from that of an adult, especially before the fontanel has fully closed. Facial proportions are also different, and will change as the child grows older.

Elderly people usually make extremely good models. They are prepared to sit patiently while you make painstaking drawings and, provided you are able to chat and draw at the same time, often enjoy the companionship coupled with the novel experience of modeling.

Detailed linework
So long as you take the trouble to make your model comfortable and arrange for regular breaks, drawing an elderly person provides you with the opportunity to spend time using linear media, such as pencil or pen and ink, for detailed studies.

Time to experiment
Here the artist has experimented with different media to convey mature, time-worn faces: black-charcoal pencil (above), soft-graphite pencil (right), and pen and ink (far right).

True representation
Because they are no longer in the first flush of youth, elderly people are always fascinating subjects to draw. An honest representation can be a dignified and very characteristic portrait.

Tone drawing
The age and character of these models has been captured tonally: wash over watercolor pencil (above left); gray pastel and charcoal (below left); straight brush-and-wash drawing (below right).

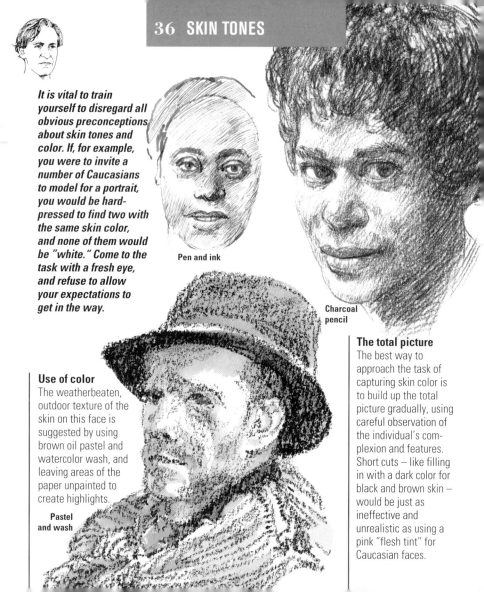

It is vital to train yourself to disregard all obvious preconceptions about skin tones and color. If, for example, you were to invite a number of Caucasians to model for a portrait, you would be hardpressed to find two with the same skin color, and none of them would be "white." Come to the task with a fresh eye, and refuse to allow your expectations to get in the way.

Pen and ink

Charcoal pencil

The total picture
The best way to approach the task of capturing skin color is to build up the total picture gradually, using careful observation of the individual's complexion and features. Short cuts – like filling in with a dark color for black and brown skin – would be just as ineffective and unrealistic as using a pink "flesh tint" for Caucasian faces.

Use of color
The weatherbeaten, outdoor texture of the skin on this face is suggested by using brown oil pastel and watercolor wash, and leaving areas of the paper unpainted to create highlights.

Pastel and wash

Color and tone
Here we see the subtleties of "black" skin created through the use of pastel and stump (right), graphite pencil (far right), oil pastel and wash with scratched highlights (below), and straightforward brush drawing with washes (below right).

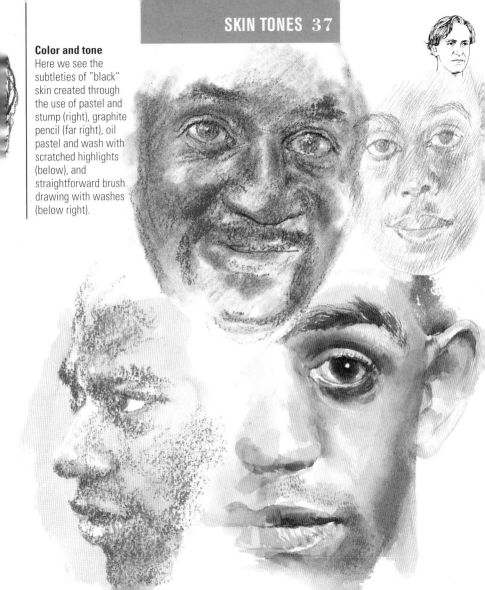

From these drawings we are able to recognize a number of ethnic groups, simply because the artist has managed to convey the genuine characteristics of the individuals she chose as models.

Pen and ink
Delicate pen cross-hatching contrasts pleasantly with watercolor washes.

Brush drawing
Brown washes are overlaid with delicate, brush-drawn linework (below).

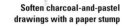

Soften charcoal-and-pastel drawings with a paper stump

Colored charcoal
The textured paper suggests reflected light in this tonal study in charcoal (right).

Graphite pencil
A similar hatched style of drawing, this time using a relatively soft pencil (below).

Watercolor pencil
After the features have been freely drawn with pencil, the skin tone and dark hair are implied with lively washes (below right).

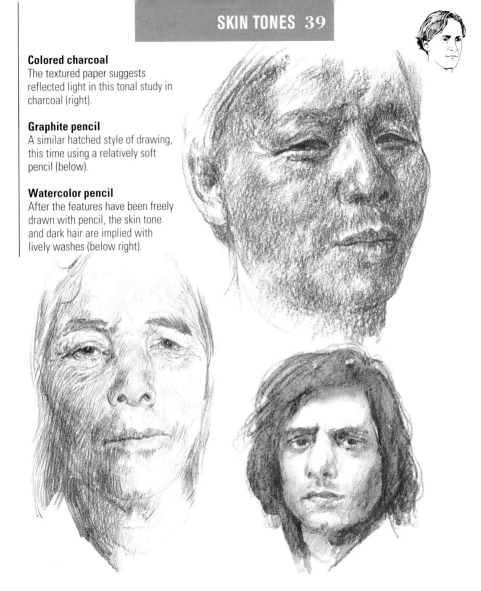

There are a number of reasons why you might include a person's hands in a portrait. Perhaps there may be a particular mannerism that characterizes your model, or you might wish to use recognizable body language to suggest a certain mood or emotion.

Charcoal

Colored pencil

Adding atmosphere
A hand that catches the light adds an element of drama to this face drawn in deep shadow (above).

Deep in thought
A simple hand gesture implies an unmistakably pensive mood (left).

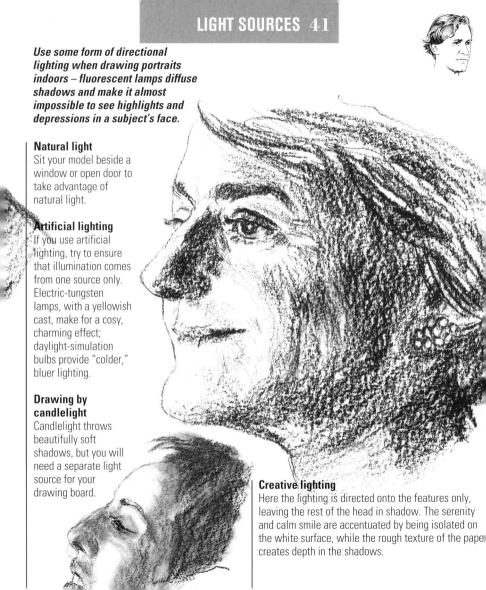

Use some form of directional lighting when drawing portraits indoors – fluorescent lamps diffuse shadows and make it almost impossible to see highlights and depressions in a subject's face.

Natural light
Sit your model beside a window or open door to take advantage of natural light.

Artificial lighting
If you use artificial lighting, try to ensure that illumination comes from one source only. Electric-tungsten lamps, with a yellowish cast, make for a cosy, charming effect; daylight-simulation bulbs provide "colder," bluer lighting.

Drawing by candlelight
Candlelight throws beautifully soft shadows, but you will need a separate light source for your drawing board.

Creative lighting
Here the lighting is directed onto the features only, leaving the rest of the head in shadow. The serenity and calm smile are accentuated by being isolated on the white surface, while the rough texture of the paper creates depth in the shadows.

Facial expressions are the epitome of body language. Most of the time, you will be trying to capture subtle grimaces, or even the angle at which your model holds his or her head. But sometimes it is enjoyable to go for more extreme and active expressions.

Freely applied watercolor washes

Black crayon

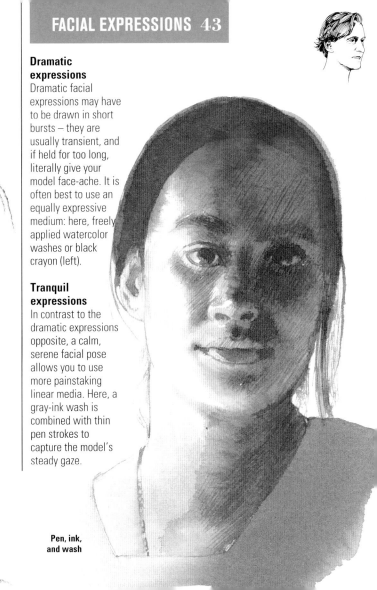

Dramatic expressions

Dramatic facial expressions may have to be drawn in short bursts – they are usually transient, and if held for too long, literally give your model face-ache. It is often best to use an equally expressive medium: here, freely applied watercolor washes or black crayon (left).

Tranquil expressions

In contrast to the dramatic expressions opposite, a calm, serene facial pose allows you to use more painstaking linear media. Here, a gray-ink wash is combined with thin pen strokes to capture the model's steady gaze.

Pen, ink, and wash

Unless you ask your models to wear particular clothes, what they choose for themselves is an expression of individual identity and taste. Headgear is particularly relevant to drawing portraits, since it inevitably becomes a major feature of the drawing.

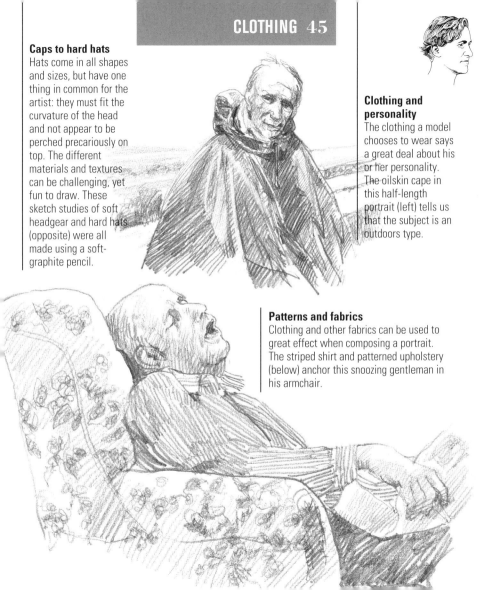

Caps to hard hats
Hats come in all shapes and sizes, but have one thing in common for the artist: they must fit the curvature of the head and not appear to be perched precariously on top. The different materials and textures can be challenging, yet fun to draw. These sketch studies of soft headgear and hard hats (opposite) were all made using a soft-graphite pencil.

Clothing and personality
The clothing a model chooses to wear says a great deal about his or her personality. The oilskin cape in this half-length portrait (left) tells us that the subject is an outdoors type.

Patterns and fabrics
Clothing and other fabrics can be used to great effect when composing a portrait. The striped shirt and patterned upholstery (below) anchor this snoozing gentleman in his armchair.

You might be forgiven for believing that drawing is already difficult enough to demand all your attention. However, all artists develop little tricks that work for them for a time, but then become clichéd. A certain amount of experimentation is always refreshing.

White on black

Drawing with white pencil on dark paper is a good way to wean yourself off tracing around shapes with lines, instead of drawing marks that really describe three dimensions. With this exercise, you have to draw the highlights not the shadows – a complete reversal of standard practice.

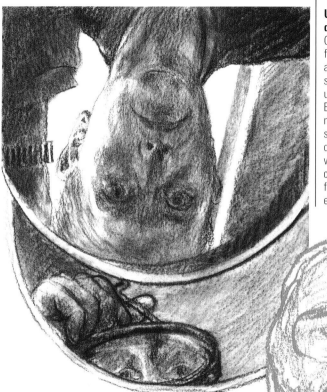

Upside-down drawing
One way to escape from preconceptions about your face is to see yourself from an unfamiliar viewpoint. By arranging two mirrors so she could see herself upside down, the artist drew what she saw – the concentration needed for this explains her expression!

Drawing wronghanded
If you are right-handed, drawing with your left hand reminds you to look carefully at what you are trying to put down on paper. You can't help but admire the freshness inherent in this wronghanded red-pastel drawing.

You are your own best model, willing to sit at a moment's notice for free, and – hopefully – not upset if the artist produces a portrait that is unflattering. (The famous society portraitist, John Singer Sargent, once observed, "Every time I paint a portrait, I lose a friend.")

Experimentation

Another advantage of self-portraiture is that you have plenty of time to experiment with viewpoints, lighting, and different media. Here the artist drew herself, using three grades of charcoal pencil in three-quarter shadow. The dramatic lighting serves to accentuate the artist's distinctive cheek shape, a feature shared by many of her family.

Photographs make acceptable artist's reference material, provided you use them as you would use sketches, and not as an end in themselves. A good photograph is a creative two-dimensional image in its own right, and a straight copy is not going to bring anything to it; the photograph will probably be better.

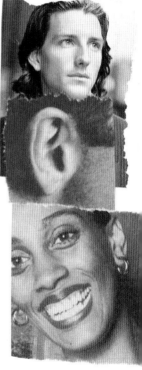

When to use photographs
Photographs are especially useful in situations when there is very little time for drawing – such as when working with an active child, for example. Always try to make a few sketches at the same time, to augment your photographic record, and take as many shots as possible from different viewpoints during the session. The sketches will tell you something about the three-dimensional nature of the living person, while the photographs will capture the things you may not be able to include in quick sketches, such as textures and small details.

Lens distortion
Wide-angle lenses tend to distort human features, particularly when used for close-ups.

Beware of distortion
When taking your own reference photographs, don't forget that camera lenses distort, particularly wide-angle lenses. This type of lens is often fitted as standard in instant and automatic cameras, and your drawings will need adjusting accordingly.

Building a reference library
If you are interested in particular themes for your drawings, it pays to build a reference library, comprising your own photographs and cuttings from newspapers and magazines, so that you will have a rich variety of viewpoints, lighting conditions, and people to draw upon.

Reference library
Use images from newspapers and magazines to build up a picture library.

BASIC

ESSENTIALS

The only essential equipment you need for drawing is a pencil and a piece of paper. But, as your experience grows and your skills develop, you will hopefully discover your own drawing style. As this happens, you will probably develop a preference for using particular art materials. Throughout this book you will have seen references to a variety of art terms, materials, and techniques, some of which may be new to you. The following is a glossary of useful information that relates to the artwork featured in this book.

MATERIALS

Graphite pencil

The common, "lead" pencil, available in a variety of qualities and price ranges. The graphite core (lead) is encased in wood and graded, from softness to hardness: 9B is very, very soft, and 9H is very, very hard. HB is the middle-grade, everyday, writing pencil. The H-graded pencils are mostly used for technical work. For freehand drawing work, start around the 2B mark.

Colored pencil

A generic term for all pencils with a colored core. There is an enormous variety of colors and qualities available. They also vary in softness and hardness, but, unlike graphite pencils, this is seldom indicated on the packet.

Watercolor pencil

As above, except water-soluble and capable of creating a variety of "painterly" effects, by either wetting the tip of the pencil or working on dampened paper.

Charcoal

Charcoal drawing sticks, made from charred willow or vine twigs, are available in three grades: soft, medium, and hard. Soft charcoal, which is very powdery, is ideal for blending and smudging; the harder varieties are better for linear drawing. When made into pencils, charcoal is cleaner and more controllable.

Pastels

Drawing sticks made by blending colored pigments with chalk or clay and bound with gum. This type of pastel is relatively soft and brittle. Oil pastels, made using an animal-fat binder, are stronger and less crumbly. Both types of pastels are available in a very wide range of colors and tones, as are pastel pencils.

Drawing ink
There is a variety of inks available, from water-soluble, writing (fountain-pen or calligraphy) inks to thick, permanent, and waterproof drawing inks. India ink is a traditional drawing ink: it is waterproof and very dense, drying with an interesting, shiny surface. The inks are available in many colors, and can be thinned down with distilled water for creating washes.

Steel-nib (dip) pen
The old-fashioned, dip-in-the-inkwell pen; a worthy and versatile drawing instrument. You may want to experiment with nibs for thickness and flexibility, but just a single nib can make a variety of line widths, as you alter the pressure on the pen.

Paper
Varies enormously in type, quality, texture, manufacture, and price. Paper is graded from smooth to rough, and is either smooth (hot-pressed, or HP), medium (cold-pressed, or CP), or rough. The smoothness or roughness of a paper is known as the "tooth." For example, the tooth of a watercolor paper is generally more marked, and rougher than that of a cartridge paper for drawing. The tooth of a paper will influence the way that a medium reacts to it.

Paper stump
Strip of paper twisted into a narrow cone. The point is used to blend and soften charcoal or pastel.

TERMS

Drybrush
A drawing effect created by using a sparsely-loaded brush, often with watercolor, or dry, fiber-tip pen. Drybrush allows the texture of the paper or any drawing beneath to show through.

Mixed media
A drawing made using two or more materials, for example, graphite pencil used with watercolor pencil.

Line drawing
A drawing made up purely of lines, with no attempt to indicate shadow or darker areas through shading or hatching.

Brush drawing
A drawing made solely with a brush.

Wash
The free application of a transparent color or tone to a drawing, usually applied with a paintbrush.

Shading
An indication of shadow or dark areas in a drawing, made by darkening the overall surface of the area, often by rubbing.

Tone
The prevailing shade in a drawing, and its comparative dullness or brightness.

Highlights
The lighter points in a drawing. These are generally the points where light strikes an object, such as a reflection in an eye, or on a surface.

Hatching
An illusion of shadow, tone, or texture in a drawing, indicated by closely drawn lines.

Crosshatching
An illusion of darker shadows, tones, or textures, indicated by overlayering hatched lines at differing angles to each other.

Parallel hatching
Shadows, tones, or textures, indicated by drawing lines next to one another.

Dot and stipple
An illusion of darker shadows, tones, or textures, indicated by small dots, usually made with the pointed tip of the drawing instrument.

POSSIBILITIES

INDEX OF POSSIBILITIES There are many ways of looking at the world, and there are as many ways of interpreting it. Art and creativity in drawing are not just about "correctness" or only working in a narrow, prescribed manner; they are about the infinite ways of seeing a three-dimensional object and setting it down.

In the earlier sections of this book, the consultant artist demonstrated some of her different approaches to drawing a specific subject. Her examples show how she has developed a personal way of seeing and setting down faces.

The following section of images is intended to further help you discover and develop your own creativity. It is an index of possibilities: an indication of just some of the inventive and inspirational directions that creative artists have taken, and continue to take. This visual glossary demonstrates how the same subject can be treated in a variety of ways, and how different cultures and artistic conventions can affect treatments.

In every culture and age, symbols and simplified images are vital factors in communication. The earliest cave drawings reduce the forms of men and animals to the basics, and tell an immediate story; similarly, modern advertising campaigns and computer-based, corporate trademarks depend on our instant recognition of simplified forms. The graphic images in this section show how the artist's eye and hand can produce universally understood forms in all human societies.

A major part of artistic and technical development is being aware of, and open to, possibilities from outside your chosen sphere. To that end, the images in this section use a wide variety of materials and techniques. They may not all be pure "drawing," but each one expands the boundaries of what is possible, and provides new ways of seeing and interpreting faces.

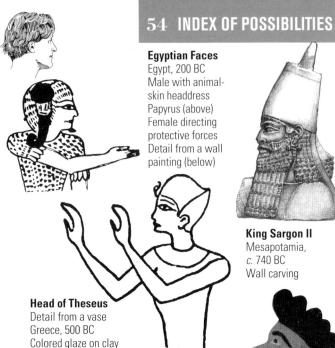

Egyptian Faces
Egypt, 200 BC
Male with animal-skin headdress
Papyrus (above)
Female directing protective forces
Detail from a wall painting (below)

King Sargon II
Mesapotamia,
c. 740 BC
Wall carving

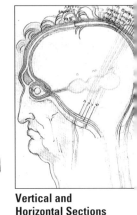

Vertical and Horizontal Sections of the Head
Sectional drawing of the layers of the skull and brain, compared with an onion
Leonardo da Vinci (1452–1519)
Italy, *c.* 1500
Pen and ink

Head of Theseus
Detail from a vase
Greece, 500 BC
Colored glaze on clay

Male Rider
Detail from a burial chamber
Siberia, 7th–2nd century BC
Pazyryk felt

Physiognomia
Engravings used to demonstrate the belief that the shape and features of the face dictate character
Barthélemy Coclès (*fl.* 16th century)
France, *c.* 1550
Engravings

Mona Lisa (La Gioconda)
Leonardo da Vinci (1452–1519)
Italy, 1503
Oil on panel

Queen Elizabeth I
Attributed to George Gower (*fl.* 16th century)
England, *c.* 1550
Oil on panel

The Last Judgement (left)
Giotto di Bondone (*c.* 1270–1337)
Italy, *c.* 1310
Fresco

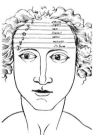

Astrological Correspondences
Diagrams to establish character and future through individual facial features
Jérôme Cardan (*fl.* 16th century)
France, *c.* 1500
Engraving

The Artist's Mother
Albrecht Dürer (1471–1538)
Germany, 1514
Charcoal

Studies of Prostitutes
Henri de Toulouse-Lautrec (1864–1901)
France, 1894
Colored chalk and pencil

Self-portrait
Aubrey Beardsley
(1872–98)
England, c. 1894
Pen and ink

Face of Fruit and Vegetables
Paul Flindt
(1592–1618)
Germany, 1611
Pen and ink

Nakamura Utaemon III
Fan-shaped portrait
Katsushika Hokusai
(1760–1849)
Japan, 1825
Engraving

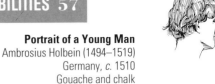

Portrait of a Young Man
Ambrosius Holbein (1494–1519)
Germany, *c.* 1510
Gouache and chalk

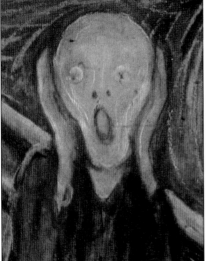

The Scream
Edvard Munch (1863–1944)
Norway, 1893
Oil, tempera, and pastel

Joseph Roulin
Vincent van Gogh
(1853–90)
France, 1888
Pen and ink

**The Three
Hierarchs**
Icon
Romania, *c.* 1800
Oil on glass

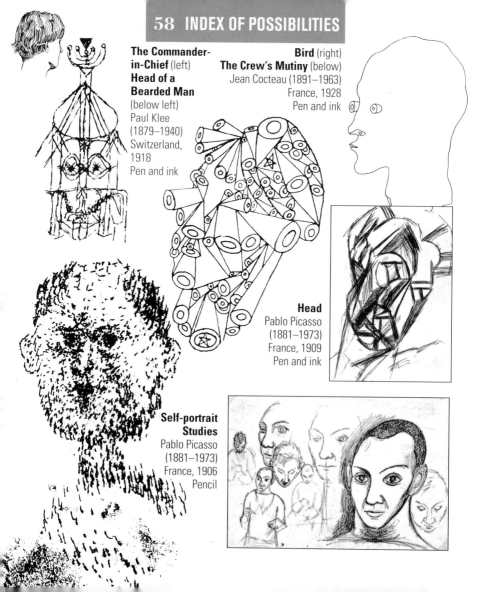

The Commander-in-Chief (left)
Head of a Bearded Man (below left)
Paul Klee
(1879–1940)
Switzerland, 1918
Pen and ink

Bird (right)
The Crew's Mutiny (below)
Jean Cocteau (1891–1963)
France, 1928
Pen and ink

Head
Pablo Picasso
(1881–1973)
France, 1909
Pen and ink

Self-portrait Studies
Pablo Picasso
(1881–1973)
France, 1906
Pencil

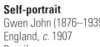

Self-portrait
Gwen John (1876–1939)
England, c. 1907
Pencil

Xenia Noelle Lowinsky
Eric Gill (1882–1940)
England, 1924
Woodcut

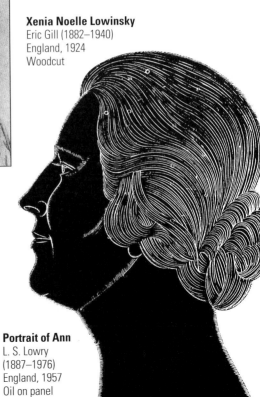

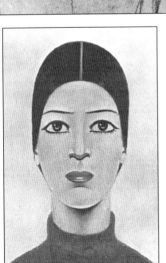

Portrait of Ann
L. S. Lowry
(1887–1976)
England, 1957
Oil on panel

Self-portrait
Fernand Léger (1881–1955)
France, 1930. Pen and ink

Head of a Fisherman
Max Pechstein (1881–1955)
Germany, 1922. Woodcut

Three Drawing Techniques
Henri Matisse
(1869–1954)

P. C. (top)
France, 1947
Charcoal
Monique Mercier
(middle)
France, 1951
Brush and ink
L. D. (bottom)
France, 1937
Pen and ink

Indian Deity
Window sticker
England, 1994
Litho print on self-
adhesive plastic

Henrietta Moraes
(right)
Francis Bacon
(1909–93)
England, 1969
Oil on canvas

Pink Marilyn
(below left)
Andy Warhol
(1930–87)
USA, 1964
Silkscreen on canvas

Self-portrait
(below right) Barbara
Hepworth (1903–75)
England, 1950
Oil and pencil

**Jacques de Bascher
de Beaumarchais**
David Hockney (b. 1937)
England, 1973
Colored crayon

The Young Gossip
Ross Wilson (b. 1957)
N. Ireland, 1990
Charcoal and
pen and ink

From Memory
Drawing made with
eyes closed (left)
Pen and ink
Collage Face
Found objects
(below left)
Gigol Atler
(b. 1946)
England, 1992

Hope and Optimism
John Muafangejo
(1943–87)
Namibia, 1984
Linocut (below right)

Musical Faces
Advertisement for
radio valves
England, c. 1930
Scratched-out image

**Nick-Nack
Paddywack**
Peter B.J. Anderson
(b. 1969)
England, 1994
Pen, ink, and gouache

**Afro-Caribbean
Faces**
Hair-care
product packaging
USA, 1994
Litho-printed carton

Colonel Sanders
© KFC ®
USA, 1990s
Litho-printed carton

This is Eva
Heloise Jennings (b. 1970)
Spain, 1978.
Pencil and colored crayon

CONTRIBUTORS AND CONSULTANTS

Contributing artist

Valerie Wiffen's earliest memory is of drawing a picture on the sole of her kiddy shoe with a spent match. She is a graduate of the Painting School at the Royal College of Art, and holds the Diploma in Adult and Continuing Education from London University. Currently Program Manager for Art and Design at Hackney Community College, London, she also exhibits frequently at the Royal Academy, and regularly undertakes portrait commissions. She is a contributing artist to *Ways of Drawing the Human Figure* in this series.

Educational consultant

Carolynn Cooke gained a degree in Graphic Design from Canterbury College of Art and a Postgraduate Certificate of Education from Leicester University. She has been teaching art for over twenty years, and is currently Head of Art and Design at Impington Village College, near Cambridge, England.

SOURCES/BIBLIOGRAPHY

In addition to the original artwork shown in this book, many books, journals, printed sources, galleries, and collections have been consulted in the preparation of this work and the Index of Possibilities. The author and editors would like to express their thanks to all artists who have contributed to the preparation of this volume. The following will be found to make useful and pleasurable reading in connection with the history and development of the art of drawing faces:

Andy Warhol: A Retrospective,
Museum of Modern Art, New York, 1989
The Art of the Felt Maker, M. Burkett,
Abbot Hall Art Gallery, 1979
The Artist as Reporter, P. Hogarth, Reinhold, 1967
The Atlas of Early Man,
J. Hawkes, St. Martin's Press, 1976
The Collected Drawings of Aubrey Beardsley,
A. Symons, Crown Publishers, 1971
The Complete Tadanori Yokoo, Art Now Tokyo, 1971
David Hockney: Dessins et Oeuvres,
Galerie Claude Bernard, 1975
Edvard Munch, U. Bischoff, Benedikt Taschen, 1993
The End of Expressionism,
J. Weirstein, University of Chicago Press, 1990
Eric Gill: The Engravings, C. Skelton, Herbert Press, 1990
F. Léger, G. Néret, Cromwell Editions London, 1993
Gwen John: An Interior Life,
C. Langdale and D. Jenkins, Phaidon, 1985
I Was Lonelyness: The Complete Graphic Works of John Muafangejo,
O. Levinson, Museum of Modern Art, Oxford, 1990
Inner Visions: German Prints from the Age of Expressionism,
Portland Art Museum, 1991
Japanese Graphic Art, L. Hajek, Gallery Press, 1976
Leonardo da Vinci, Yale University Press, 1989
Muck Island,
R. Wilson and A. Rice, Moongate Publications, 1990
The National Portrait Gallery Collection,
NPG Publications, 1988
Old Master Portrait Drawings, J. Spero, Dover, 1990
Pablo Picasso: Genius of the Century,
C. Warncke and I. Walther, Benedikt Taschen, 1992